The Fruits of Inclus
A Smart Business Guide to Creating a Sustainable Diversity and Inclusion Program

By
Dr. Linda Jackson Burrs

TM 2007

Fruits of Inclusion Graphic and Second Generation Diversity Training logo is trademarked ™ to Dr. Linda J. Burrs and Step Up to Success! Miamisburg, OH 45342.
Designing a Diversity and Inclusion Strategy image ™ is trademarked to Dr. Linda J. Burrs and Step Up To Success!
Cover design by Mur ge Murals and Decorative Paintings, Springboro, OH

Library of Congress Control Number: 2007905830
ISBN 13:978-0-615-15426-8

Table of Contents

Table of Contents—*continued*

Foreword

For more than ten years, diversity has been a hot business topic. A tremendous amount of time and money has been spent defining, discussing, and more recently, debating the value of diversity – and more recently inclusion.

The notion of inclusion is not a new one for us. Our nation was founded on the principle of inclusion. The War Between the States – the Civil War, was about inclusion. While the going since the Civil War has not been without challenges and setbacks, it certainly set the stage for our present day inclusion efforts – and such a foundation is certainly apropos for a nation of immigrants.

In her book, The Fruits of Inclusion™, Dr. Burrs clearly articulates the difference between diversity and inclusion. She focuses on why both of these principles must co-exist and recognizes the importance of diverse work groups. But, she does not stop there; she outlines a plan of action to achieve inclusive relationships. Throughout the book you are guided through the steps necessary to assess your present state and then steps are outlined to help you develop your desired state – inclusive teams. Her focus and discussions on the importance of communication and leadership create a clear understanding of how these principles are key to the success of inclusion strategies.

This reference tool illustrates how to make diversity and inclusion changes that "stick". The book: The Fruits of Inclusion™ is a valuable tool for anyone trying to develop inclusive teams through sound leadership and communication principles. I applaud Dr. Burrs' insight in the development of this guide and encourage you to seriously use this training and development tool!

Myra Kennedy Fincher
Chief, Diversity and EEOC
WPAFB

Copyright 2007 Dr. Linda Burrs and/or Step Up To Success!

The Fruits of Inclusion: A Smart Business Guide to Creating a Sustainable Diversity and Inclusion Program

Preface

Oh no… here we go again… another diversity initiative … another diversity book… another diversity program. Sound familiar? Not this time! This is the *Second Generation Diversity Training©*… the time is now, and it is long past due. Second generation diversity training has arrived and is better than ever. Diversity is about **ALL** of us, not just some of us. We are all diverse and as such, we need to learn how to be inclusive and more responsive to each other. Diversity training should never be about blame, shame, or making others feel guilty. Real diversity training is about learning how to respond to each other's differences in ways that helps us individually and collectively move beyond our personal notions of what is right and wrong and what is truth.

Second generation diversity training© (SGDT©) is about creating cultures of excellence through the practices of inclusion. It is about developing skills that offer everyone an opportunity to have a seat and a say. Second generation diversity training is about how to explore truths beyond our normal conditioning so we may all enjoy the fruits of hard work, innovative practices, and creative energy that bring the very best into the workplace and into society. SGDT© is about building the type of skills that make our workplaces havens of energy, excitement and commitment versus places of fear, entropy, and doubt. If you want employees waking up WANTING to come to work versus HAVING to come to work, read on.

Those who succeed in finding their way through the maze of globalization, breakthrough technology, and higher order thinking will be the ones who embrace diversity in its truest sense and in all of its forms. These unique visionaries will be the ones who see and understand the impending collision course between the forces of economic stability and the moral responsibility of organizational unity by establishing, embracing, and supporting a culture of inclusion. The remarkable thing about diversity is its striking ability to bridge differences in a way that supports the inner connectivity of us all.

There are some estimates that there are more than 10 million insect species, 500,000 varieties of plant life and more than 6 billion people residing on our planet Earth. The question is not should we support diversity, the question is how can we best define, support and shape policies, attitudes, and programs that help individuals see themselves as a part of a greater system of diversity... a complex system of interconnectedness, a diverse system of inclusion in which we all belong and reside.

There is no type of diversity that does not include every group of people. Diversity is not about a select few or one group over another. The real power of diversity is in its ability to positively change us all for the better.

Introduction

Diversity is not a new concept or idea nor is the need for designing useful diversity strategies a novel thought. What is different is the critical state in which organizations find themselves. Never have organizations been in such crises as they are now in leader-follower relationships, ability to solve problems, and to compete for talent just to name a few organizational issues. As the need to develop and implement inclusion programs that are useful and sustainable in a world where differences are more important to an organization's success than ever before, developing strategies that are meaningful and practical, but realistic and doable are of utmost importance.

For years diversity training focused on the differences of race and gender while other gifts went unnoticed and under-utilized. Too often we did not take the time to figure out how to get beyond the visible differences in order to take advantage of the differences that could help us increase our profitability, improve our organization's performance, decrease conflict and improve our ability to communicate with each other.

Diversity is the seed and inclusion is the fruit. Most seeds don't make it past germination because proper nurturing in the form of skill development has not taken place in order for the fruit of inclusion to be adequately nourished so it can fully grow and blossom. I have heard leaders say for years, well, we tried diversity and it just did not work. We hired a couple of minorities and they didn't work out.

When the extent of one's diversity program is hiring a couple of minorities, it is astonishing an organization's diversity strategy works at all. Here's the truth of the matter. The term "diversity" carries so much baggage that the word itself has become almost crippling to diversity in its truest sense. Where we have missed the real message in diversity is where we have placed our values. We invest in assets. We don't invest in liabilities. When we value diversity, we will invest in providing our assets (the people in your employ) the skills they need to successfully bear the fruit you want them to bear.

When considering the many ways we are different and how fears, biases, and lack of understanding of our differing values, expectations, beliefs, and assumptions lead us down paths we never thought we would take, it is a wonder anyone gets anything done. From the start, if we view diversity or each other as a liability, then the organization starts from a position of deficiency. This is why many diversity programs fail. It is because they are not set up from inception to succeed.

Diversity and inclusion are NOT about creating a place for some while taking another's place away. They are NOT social programs or a remake of a quota system designed to meet a government standard. Diversity is about making our differences work for all of us. Diversity and inclusion should be a strategic initiative designed to improve organizational effectiveness and business performance to ensure economic success for everyone, and in order for diversity to work, inclusion must have a chance to germinate and grow. For inclusion to have a chance to evolve and grow, trust must be planted into the heart and soul of the organization's culture. There will be more on this concept later.

There are some who argue diversity and inclusion are simply rhetoric. I would argue these individuals may be too focused solely on race and gender and more often than not, my experience with these individuals suggest they are not open to a broader perspective of what the words diversity and inclusion truly mean. I also suggest opponents of diversity and inclusion may not know how to genuinely embrace the concepts of diversity and inclusion in a way that brings understanding beyond their normal conditioning.

We are all diverse and it is long past time for the second generation of diversity training to begin. Second generation diversity is a skill building series of programs that helps organizations move beyond the traditional barriers encountered from being diverse.

Here are just a few of the many types of diversity:

- Personality
- Communication
- Leadership style
- Learning styles / teaching styles
- Economic
- Cultural
- Work styles
- Perception
- Geographic
- Language
- Social
- Education
- Privilege

You will notice age, race, gender and sexual orientation are not listed. These differences were purposefully excluded. When society remains focused just on these *visible forms* of diversity to the exclusion of the *invisible forms* of diversity, we will continue to miss opportunities to move beyond our current state. The invisible forms of diversity are what give us our character, our essence, and our most significant insights into how we view and live in this world. Visible diversity is often the diversity that gets in our way and prevents us from seeing and benefiting from other forms of diversity which are equally important. If you look at me and all you see is my visible diversity and allow that brief snapshot to form your opinion of me, then you have missed the opportunity to know who I am and what I have to offer. If by only focusing on my visible diversity to determine whether I am worthy of your time and attention, then again you have missed the essence of the gifts and talents I bring to the table. Second generation diversity© teaches us how to close this visible/invisible gap that often prevents us from being more inclusive.

Does this mean race, gender, and sexual orientation are not important? Of course not. What I am saying is this; diversity is about respecting, honoring, and cherishing differences regardless of hair color, weight, height, race, gender, abilities or disabilities, personality differences, thinking styles, origin of birth, geographic location, education level, or any other of the hundred ways we might be different.

Are there race and gender problems in our workplaces? Sure there are, but if we ever hope to overcome these challenges, we have to learn how to deal with them in ways that do not antagonize, harm, or take advantage through guilt, blame, or in shaming others to get what we want. This is true for all of us regardless of who we are or where we start, and to overcome these challenges we must begin by sending the real message we want others to receive.

Second generation diversity training© suggests it is time to move beyond our previous feeble attempts to control outcomes of race and gender as we consider the many issues facing us in our dealings with each other. We have to make it safe to discuss the un-discussable in ways that do not harm the integrity and spirit of another. We need each other to make our workplaces better. Digging in our heels because we think we are right only gets us sore feet.

Diversity and Inclusion – What's the Difference?

Often the terms diversity and inclusion are used interchangeably. You may be wondering if there is a difference and if so what is it? Here is a brief explanation. Diversity refers to demographic differences that distinguish one person from another. These demographic differences may be observable or unobservable. On the other hand, inclusion is a state of being that supports diversity in that inclusion enables diverse individuals and groups to function together in ways where differences are respected, gifts are valued and everyone is welcomed regardless of their diversity.

When the conditions of inclusion are effectively practiced, inclusion offers the added advantage of increased participation in decision-making, access to information, greater empowerment of employees to solve organizational problems and collaborative teamwork. Those influenced by an inclusive work environment will actively seek to remove barriers that prevent full access to employee talents. *Inclusion seeks to embrace and not merely tolerate differences.*

Why now?

Why diversity with inclusion and why now? We seem to be in crisis mode in organizations about how to deal with each other and we have been for years! It is past time for us to emerge from the darkness of name-calling and finger pointing into the light of skill development that comes with inclusion. It should be our collective goal to work together today to change tomorrow. In the words credited to Terry Tempest Williams, "The eyes of the future are looking back at us and they are praying for us to see beyond our own time." Second generation diversity training© offers infinite probabilities for success - diversity with inclusion – a testament to what we may accomplish together.

Who should use this workbook?

If you have tried unsuccessfully to initiate a diversity program in the past, try it again. Don't give up. Ask for help if you need it. If used appropriately, this workbook will help organizations of all sizes capitalize on differences through the use of inclusion so that they may focus on those tasks and responsibilities that will generate the most meaningful results.

Who should use this workbook? Any leader hoping to benefit from the many ways we are different regardless of the industry of type of organization in which you work. Churches, schools, businesses of any size, for-profits and not-for-profits, government entities, the military, teams of any size, groups of any kind may all benefit from the information that will be found in these pages. The guide was written in phases so as not to overwhelm the reader with monumental tasks. Read some… think some… write some… do some. As you go through the workbook, you will find yourself reflecting on what you read and you may want to write down your thoughts or talk them out. You may even want to share your thoughts with a group or a team. That is perfectly okay and is generally a great way to get good dialogue going that usually produces extraordinary results.

How to use this guide

When it comes to designing a sound and useful diversity and inclusion strategy, one size does NOT fit all! This workbook is simply a guide. The purpose of this book is to provide the reader guidance by offering thoughtful starter questions and unique approaches in a workbook style.

The models provided present a framework around which you may build a strategy that will allow you to take your organization's unique characteristics into consideration as you build a useful strategy. Methodologies discussed in this guidebook are intended to assist you in developing second generation diversity and inclusion strategies with training programs that teach skills needed to support inclusion skill development.

Even though this book was written in four phases, each of these sections may be considered individually as well as a collective work. Here are some guiding tips to optimize the benefits from reading this book.

Most organizations already have sales strategies, product development or marketing strategies and even human resource strategies already in place. These in-place programs provide a template from which to begin. For far too many organizations, you are beginning with a blank slate for developing real diversity and inclusion programs that can have long-term and long lasting effects.

Here are some important do's and don'ts:

**** **IMPORTANT** ***

- **Do** read the questions as thought starters and not as a list of things you must do all at one time. **Don't** allow yourself to become overwhelmed by the potential size of the task.

- **Do** take one step at a time unless you are comfortable taking two. Concentrate on what you may realistically accomplish. Change takes time and remember, even if the change you **CAN** make seems miniscule to others, it could be monumental to you and may be the most significant effort you take to begin the journey of being more inclusive. **Don't** get derailed by focusing on what you can't bring yourself to grapple with just yet.

- **Do** engage in purposeful activities that reinforce your commitment to stick with the values of inclusion. **Don't** allow your fears or lack of enthusiasm toward inclusiveness dissuade your grand intentions toward making inclusion work for you and your organization.

- **Do** keep in mind that for some, embracing the concept of the *fruits of inclusion*™ is a life changing event, so take one day at a time and enjoy your successes. Success produces its own brand of optimism. **Don't** ever give up.

Take some time to reflect and ponder on the different phases or steps. If you start to feel overwhelmed, stop reading and figure out why you are experiencing these emotions or thoughts. Deal with what you are feeling but do not give up on what you are hoping to accomplish. Don't ever give up on the goal of becoming the difference that will make a difference.

It is the sincerest desire of the author that the readers of this work will become participants in the *birth of inclusion* by creating the type of future where differences help us more than hurt us, where trusting relationships are more common than mean-spirited disingenuousness, and honest dialogue has replaced the fear of saying no to the status quo.

Let's begin.

Phase I - Preparing for Inclusion

Before any leader ever begins designing a diversity and inclusion strategy, they must take the time to understand why they are undertaking this initiative. Diversity must be worth something to the stakeholders accepting this responsibility. Diversity must mean something to the leader, employees, the organization, and all of its other stakeholders. This meaning must be clearly and succinctly communicated to the members of the organization over and over again.

Take some time to reflect on these questions:

- What future do you want for your organization?
- What is the virtue of practicing diversity and inclusion?
- How do you view diversity? Do you value the concept as an asset or a liability?
- What are the core values and principles that guide this organization?
- Why are you considering this strategy?
- What is the business case for doing this?
- What is the ethical principle guiding you as you consider this strategy?
- What is the greater good here?
- What type of relationships do you have or do you want to have in your organization?
- Is this the right strategy for this organization right now?
- As leader, am I personally ready to take on this challenge?
- How far are you willing to take this diversity and inclusion strategy?
- Where is this organization on the issue of trust?
- Can you be present when others need you or challenge you on this issue?
- How will you frame this issue as an organization? As a community?
- What is in this strategy for the organization?
- What is in this strategy for employees?
- What is in this strategy for all stakeholders?
- Am I able to commit my organization's resources to this strategy over the long haul?

Notes on thoughts

Diversity is not just something to do to make sure everyone in the organization feels warm and fuzzy about working there. It has been repeatedly suggested a meaningful diversity and inclusion program is a business strategy designed to make a steady, significant, and sound financial and cultural impact to an organization's bottom line and organizational climate. In other words, being a well managed, diverse organization should equal financial excellence and upstanding organizational character not only to customers in your respective markets but also in how employees feel about working there.

Creating a culture of inclusion could signal to your customers that your organization is committed to providing the highest level of service possible. In an age of more educated and discerning customers who have little brand loyalty, differentiating your organization may well position you to become not only a reputable and good corporate citizen poised to increase profits, but it may also distinguish you as an innovative problem solver.

A well planned diversity strategy is not just about putting together an economic business case. It should also serve as a moral compass for creating the type of world in which you want to live. A CEO of a major organization (well known for their diversity efforts) was asked by a student, if diversity did NOT impact his bottom line, would he still do what he was doing? The CEO reviewed what he had already said but the young man was persistent and asked him again, if diversity did not impact your bottom line, would you still do all this? The CEO tried to answer *again* but he missed the boat. Another student stood up and suggested his fellow student's question still wasn't answered. What were these students asking the CEO? They were asking him if diversity was just a business strategy or was it a heart strategy as well.

Diversity involves both the head and the heart. It is a *head thing* (business case) and a *heart thing* (emotional and psychological). If we have any hope of accepting people for who they are and not what they look like, then we have to exercise head and heart leadership. It has to be both.

Truly valuing diversity is about valuing trusting relationships. It is about honesty in dialogue with each other. It is about being willing to create the space and opportunity to criticize and say you are wrong or this could be done another way. It is about being open to seeing, doing, and making changes within the system without fear of ridicule or reprisal. This is where the real value of diversity is seen, and where inclusion encourages honest conversations. This is how individual gifts support innovative ideas, concepts and changes on behalf of the organization. This is diversity at work, fueled by the power of inclusion.

When it becomes okay to get into an honest dialogue about how to change what is being done, or how to look at a problem in a new light or offer criticism because the team or group has transcended blame, you have entered that exclusive space called *inclusion*. When you are in a place where honest conversations (not to be confused with mean-spirited discussions) has evolved and progression of thought has taken place, you will know *inclusion has born fruit*. It is now safe to reach out to others, without fear, and share ideas that serve the best interest of the organization.

As you consider the meaning behind the diversity and inclusion strategy you want to develop, take into account both the economic business case and the ethical principles guiding the decisions you are making. How might you respond to these questions?

- Who benefits most from current polices?
- Where is this organization headed?
- What does this organization look like and what will it look like after inclusion has born its fruits?
- What might it feel like to walk into this organization if you were a stranger?
- What would your customers never say about you?
- What impressions would others have looking in from the outside?
- What are your strengths?
- What do you do better than anybody else in the business?
- Where are your weaknesses hurting you strategically?
- On what are you focused?

- Where should you be focused?
- Are you building walls or bridges in your conversations? How do you know?
- Could your current policies (written or unwritten) be perceived as gateways to fearful unknowns or welcome additions?
- Do you have the skill sets to deal with differences?
- Are you communicating beneath the radar so you don't get caught saying something you shouldn't?
- Are your managers encouraging open and honest dialogue about differences?
- What does your ideal future look like?
- Is your organization comfortable where it is right now? Should it be? What do you need to do to shake things up? What can you do?
- Are your managers skilled enough to successfully deal with differences when confronted with unfamiliar situations?
- Is this an organization where risk is viewed as an essential element of success?
- Is self-empowerment encouraged?
- Is it comfortable to express dissent in this organization?
- Is *creative abrasion* accepted?
- Do you have a welcoming environment?
- Have you considered how you will measure the risk against the reward of this strategy? How will you manage this?
- Does working in this organization feel like being stuck and going nowhere? How do you know?
- Is yours a high energy organization where employees come to work fully engaged and bring their best self to work? If not, do you know why not?
- Is your organization ready and eager to change or one that is fearful of change?

Notes on thoughts

We can no longer afford to be exclusive in our behaviors and practices towards others. Exclusionary policies (written or unwritten) harm everyone and the organization by marginalizing the inherent potential available in every employee, thus creating under-developed organizations, non-productive teams, entropy-riddled cultures, and worst of all, a blind eye to the reality of what is truly possible when we have learned how to make our differences work for us.

Who should be involved in the development of the strategy?

Simply stated, everyone should get and stay involved; however, the most successful diversity and inclusion strategies begin with the CEO. To build a diversity strategy that has any chance of working, the program must be built from the very top with additions from other areas of the organization as the program is implemented. There is no point in even attempting to establish a program of diversity and inclusion if the highest level executive of the organization is not involved in making the program a top priority. As the President and CEO of the organization goes, so goes the organization. Just as the most senior level person is committed to sales and marketing programs, production programs, and product development programs, the CEO MUST be equally committed to their diversity and inclusion strategy and programs in order for it to be given serious consideration by the members in the organization.

Diversity and inclusion is NOT a human resources program. A diversity and inclusion program slated for success does not belong in human resources any more than a sales strategy or product development or marketing program belongs in human resources. Diversity and inclusion strategies are organizational strategies just like every other organizational objective. Relegating diversity and inclusion to human resources merely as something to do guarantees its failure. Most research studies have confirmed this to be true. Human resources may manage the strategy, but without direct and serious commitment and **visible** involvement from the top executive and the executive's team, not much will change. Failure to get serious commitment from the Chief Executive Officer is the deal breaker.

The CEO and the Executive Team

The CEO will be expected to provide: consistent and frequent communication about the seriousness and permanence of the strategy; meaningfulness of the program, resources dedicated to the success of the program, and the expectation for the full cooperation of every manager, leader, employee, vendor, and all stakeholders of the organization in order to create a culture of expectation that inclusion will be the norm.

For this to happen, incentive programs will need to be developed for senior and mid-level managers to recognize and reward the types of actions and behaviors that warrant repetition. Likewise, sanctions should be designed that acknowledge and deter actions and behaviors that must be stopped so that inclusion has a fair and safe opportunity to develop in the organization's culture. Like rewards and recognition, sanctions should be meaningful and useful. Examples of helpful sanctions are personal coaching or additional training that will lead to the development of *inclusion competence* or other training that would be useful. In the event these measures are not successful or fail to lead to a positive change, stronger measures must be considered.

Change takes places when inclusion gets the serious *hands-on involvement* from executive-level officers and receives the resources needed to make it work. This is when inclusion will begin to germinate and take root in the organization's culture.

- Are you ready for the level of commitment that is necessary for your diversity and inclusion strategy?
- How will you demonstrate this level of **continued** dedication to the diversity and inclusion strategy you are preparing to design?

Notes on thoughts

Middle Managers

Research suggests mid-level managers most often have significant influence in shaping how change happens in organizations. These managers are most likely able to get new standards established, new processes and procedures implemented, and they are able to create the type of work environment where inclusion may either thrive or *die on the vine*. In other words, this level of management makes things happen. Getting this group involved and getting their buy-in for strategies that impact their day-to-day work space is critical. Answering the question, what's in it for me and my team is going to make a huge difference for this group of individuals. Ask yourself these questions about your middle managers:

- How will you respond to your middle managers or team leaders?
- How will you get mid-level management's buy-in?
- What resources are you willing to commit to their group's development to ensure their commitment and success in this strategy?
- What message do you want them sending their employees?

Notes on thoughts

Employees

In every organization, in every industry, the psychological contract between employers and employees has changed. Changes in economic conditions, markets and in how work is done have caused the psychological contract between followers and the organization to be rewritten. This shift has caused a lack of basic trust between employers and employees and because of this deficit in trust, work relationships are lacking in commitment and energy. The fear of engaging in open and honest dialogue precludes inclusive relationships. There is much at stake for employees and managers. There is even more to learn and greater still to let go of in order to change the climate of the organization. Consider these questions:

- What is the real message that must be communicated to employees about this strategy?
- What is in it for them?
- What communication program should be developed and by whom?
- What media would best serve to communicate the message?
- How often should the message go out?
- What are the potential negative responses you could get back?
- Since the bond or psychological contract between employer and employee has changed, how do you build the trust back into the relationship?
- How will you respond to positive and negative feedback?
- What system do you need to put in place to deal with the potential backlash?
- Can you make it safe for all employees to express themselves and work out their grievances?

Notes on thoughts

Suppliers / Vendors

Suppliers and vendors carry messages to and from your organization to others outside your company.

What messages are your suppliers and vendors sending or receiving about you?

- Do you have a supplier/vendor diversity program? Should you have one?
- What would your vendors or suppliers never say about you?
- Are you inclusive in the suppliers and vendors you use to deliver goods and services to your organization?

Community Partners

Local businesses, schools (universities, community colleges, trade or vocational schools, churches, non-profits, neighborhood councils, museums, parks, everyone) should get and stay involved in making the work of inclusion happen for everyone. When the community believes they have a stake in the outcome of your organization's success, everyone gets involved in helping you succeed. The community tends to overlook faults when they know it is not intentional or they believe you have their best interest at heart and you have demonstrated your willingness to be inclusive by developing programs that include all community partners.

Here are some examples:

- Scholarships/Internships (i.e., students with disabilities or different lifestyles, charter schools and suburban schools working together)
- Summer programs (i.e., low-income students, students with special challenges)
- Cooperative programs with high schools, vocational schools, trade schools, community colleges, other programs (i.e., special needs groups, charter schools)
- Incentives that recognize mentoring programs and relationships between business leaders and at risk students

In what type of programs could your organization become involved? What are the benefits and what are the risks?

Notes on thoughts

What if you find your organization is not ready for inclusion?
How do you get ready?

This is a question many have asked. There is not a one best or right response; however, here are some suggestions for helping you prepare your organization for inclusion:

- Hold leadership accountable for creating a diverse and inclusive work environment
- Create energy around the possibilities that come with inclusion by designing a statement of intent for your organization
- Publicize your commitment and goal to become an inclusive organization, team or group
- Develop diverse succession plans that cross all demographics taking into consideration community demographic data
- Assess your organization's climate and then deal with the issues you find including fear
- Partner with organizations known for their diverse and inclusive practices and ask for help
- Create an advisory board comprised of members across the organization that will develop policies and practices that reflect inclusion
- Decide if it is in your best interest to stop doing business with other organizations who do not practice inclusion
- Establish a timeline for when you want to be prepared
- Measure and evaluate your progress toward preparedness for making diversity and inclusion work in your organization

Remember, when you commit to making diversity and inclusion work for everyone, you make a pledge not only to yourself and your employees, you are making a pledge to the community at large, to your vendors and suppliers and to every stakeholder with a real interest in seeing your organization succeed.

Phase I: Preparing for Inclusion Wrap-Up

What do you want your organization's future to look like?

Are you ready for inclusion?

What do you need to change to make this happen?

Phase II - Designing the Strategy

The term strategy is defined as a plan of action(s) required in order to succeed. All of us know very well the story of Alice in Wonderland. When Alice first met the Cheshire Cat, it was during a time of confusion and at a time when Alice knew she needed some help and direction. She needed a plan. When she first met the Cheshire Cat, Alice was a bit startled. The task of designing a diversity program at first glance looks daunting. But don't let that first look deter you. Look again.

Alice asked the Cat which road she should take. She knew she needed to do something but she had no idea where to start. The Cat said the road to take depended a great deal on where she wanted to end up. Alice's response was it did not matter to her. The Cat then suggested if it doesn't matter where you end up, then it doesn't matter what road you take. All roads will all take you somewhere.

There are many leaders who wish today they had taken some time yesterday to decide where they wanted to end up before they traveled down (or up) a particular path. If it doesn't matter where you end up, then it doesn't matter whether you design a strategy that will work or not work. But if it DOES matter where you end up, then take the time to decide what road is best to travel so you set into motion a plan of action that will help you succeed in getting where you really want to go.

There are, of course, many ways to approach the development of a strategy. This is not a complicated process. First on the list: ALIGN THE DIVERSITY AND INCLUSION STRATEGY WITH THE OVERALL VISION OF THE ORGANIZATION. These two goals are NOT mutually exclusive nor should they be. Diversity strategies are just like every other functional goal except diversity and inclusion have to be aligned in some way to every functional group in the organization. Simply put, when your executive team meets to set the strategic direction for the organization, add a diversity and inclusion component to each of your business units.

Every single employee should be crystal clear how their job adds value to the overall strategy of the organization in general and diversity and inclusion specifically. The addition of a diversity and inclusion component as part of what the organization values and as a performance goal is a critical piece for ensuring the success of the diversity and inclusion strategy. It must be embedded in every function of the organization. Everyone must be responsible for making the strategy work. Every executive, every middle manager, every supervisor and every team leader should be constantly asking: How does what I do fit in with our diversity and inclusion strategy? For example, sales management should be asking, how does this sales strategy in the field fit with our diversity and inclusion strategy?

Adding management development goals as part of management performance objectives will go a long way toward holding leadership responsible for ensuring this program stays in people's peripheral vision. This helps hold every leader accountable and responsible for making the program a success and for ensuring it gets and stays on the radar screen.

Vision, Mission and Values

There are three growth stimulants within every organization that should be inseparable. These three dynamic compounds are vision, mission and values. Unless these three elements are understood and are crystal clear at the outset, the organization most likely does not have a solid sense of where they are headed, what they should be doing or what values drive them in their business.

Diversity and Inclusion Vision and Mission Statements
Creating a Diversity and Inclusion Vision Statement

This cannot be overstated. Your diversity and inclusion vision and mission statement MUST mean what it says, and say what is really meant. How many times have you heard someone say of their corporate vision and mission statement, "Oh, those words mean nothing. Those are just words on paper."

As everyone must know by now, your vision statement is where you see your future state. It is the big picture, where you see yourself as a result of the work of the strategy. Creating a vision statement takes some thought as to what is really doable and believable, not only from your position but from the position of your management team and your employees. Vision statements should inspire, captivate and give transforming power to people to change their behaviors and thoughts and redirect their energies in order to accomplish goals in support of the vision.

As you give this some thought and discussion, **envision** what your organization will look like, sound like, feel like, and work like once the work of diversity and inclusion has had an opportunity to become embedded into the culture of your organization's unique DNA. Then write down your thoughts about what it will be like to work in this type of organization. Now write out your vision statement. This is not set in stone nor should it be. Until you have a clear and compelling vision statement you know you can get support for from the organization, keep at it. You want this to be real, truthful and inspirational.

Diversity and inclusion vision statement

_____

_____

_____

_____

_____

_____

_____

_____

_____

_____

_____

_____

_____

_____

_____

_____

_____

_____

_____

_____

_____

_____

_____

_____

_____

_____

_____

Designing a Diversity and Inclusion Mission Statement

Your mission is who you are as an organization and what you do that will actually make the vision a reality. Now that you have created this amazing but realistic vision for your organization, how are you going to make this happen? What do you need to do? A mission statement tells the world what you are best in the world at doing. This statement says to the world, these are our core competencies you can count on and this is how we will deliver on our vision statement.

- Write down your core competencies
- What do you do and why you do it?
- What do you value?
    - Why should customers do business with you?
    - Why would the community trust you?
    - How do you show you care about quality, service, and relationships?

Now take these statements and form them into a 4 – 5 sentence mission statement that will explain how you will accomplish your diversity and inclusion vision.

Your diversity and inclusion mission statement

_____

_____

_____

_____

_____

_____

_____

_____

_____

_____

_____

_____

_____

_____

_____

_____

_____

_____

_____

_____

_____

Making Diversity and Inclusion Part of What the Organization Values

Values are the importance, usefulness, desirability or worthiness one attaches to an object whether real or imagined. So when your organization says they value diversity, what is the message you are sending to your stakeholders? What price is attached to the word *value* and how will you clearly communicate the importance or desirability of that value to all of your members? How will you make diversity and inclusion a value that is equal to the price you believe your organization is willing to exact in the cost to develop this strategy and implement the supporting programs? How will you ensure that everyone in your organization feels the value you state in your vision and mission are not just words on paper, but that the real value is in the actions and behaviors that are lived out in rewritten policies, building inclusive programs, and establishing day-to-day practices that will come about as a result of the values put in place by the strategy.

The word *meme* refers to an idea, a way of being, a mannerism, or a cultural value that has evolved into a way of life through an ability to transform itself into a culture's DNA. In 1976 Richard Dawkins coined this term *meme* and provided examples of memes as *catch phrases, tunes, clothing styles, and beliefs.* As some have defined diversity, there is so much negative baggage associated with the word that to try to make inclusion a positive cultural value would be futile. What can be done about this?

One idea would be to work with marketing or have an employee marketing program to come up with new ideas that best represents your organization's future.

- What are some ways to make this inclusion a *living concept* where everyone may participate in the transformation process?
- How could you use the desirability of inclusion to focus on possibilities instead of deficiencies?
- What ideas best represents the organization's purpose and sense of community?

As you think about creative ways to bring the value of inclusion deeper into the organization in a positive way, the effects of inclusion will be realized more and more as it becomes embedded into the culture.

Using the understanding of a *meme* as a framework for creating a *culture of inclusion* that is sustainable over the long term, it becomes critically important that during the design phase of the diversity strategy, leadership creates the appropriate elements of inclusion so that as the *meme of inclusion* takes hold and begins to reproduce and refine itself over time, the inclusion phenomenon produces greater *stickiness* (it is memorable), sustainability (longevity), and staging (dramatic results) giving the inclusion meme greater opportunity to survive. As *inclusiveness* become systemically integrated into the network of *practices and behaviors* within an organization, the culture experiences deep change. Once the inclusion meme reaches critical mass in acceptance as a cultural value, inclusion has been born and its influence in transforming organizational behavior has begun its work.

At this point, some questions to ask would be:

- What are your organizational values?
- How can you make inclusiveness a *way of being* in your organization?
- How might you organize around the values of diversity and inclusion?
- How could you begin practicing the virtues of diversity and inclusion?
- How do you make inclusion a *meme*?
- What are some suggestions and ideas for marketing the value of diversity and inclusion programs to your organization?
- Who are other partners you could include in your efforts to make diversity and inclusion a way of life and a value your organizational community could support? (i.e., suppliers and vendors, community partners, schools, diverse special interest groups)

- What is the sticky factor? How will you make this value memorable and meaningful?
- How will you make this value long-lasting?
- What will bring dramatic results to this value?

Notes on thoughts

_____

_____

_____

_____

_____

_____

_____

_____

_____

_____

_____

_____

_____

_____

_____

_____

_____

_____

_____

_____

_____

_____

_____

_____

_____

Designing a useable strategy

There are 4 factors to consider when designing a diversity and inclusion strategy (see Figure 1):

- What are the advantages?
- What are the disadvantages?
- What internal factors are pulling us?
- What external forces and trends are pushing us?

Designing a Diversity and Inclusion Strategy

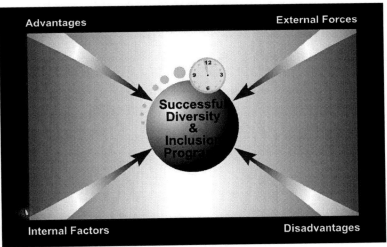

© 2007 Dr. Linda Burrs

Figure 1

Let's look at each of these factors individually.

Advantages of diversity and inclusion

Everywhere you look, people sing the praises of diversity. We consistently hear the rallying cry: We need more diversity. Diversity is good. Diversity helps us. This guide wasn't designed to argue against these points. It is designed to help the reader flush out the reasons behind WHY developing a diversity and inclusion strategy is the RIGHT strategy to pursue for your organization. There are some advantages for designing a well-planned and well-structured diversity and inclusion program. Some advantages are:

Differing data points offer opportunities for:

- Innovative problem solving
- Creative strategies that improve one's competitive position in the market
- Improvements in the product development cycle because employees at all levels of the organization feel included and therefore have a greater stake in the outcome of the organization's success
- Reducing the stress associated with risk aversion because buy-in from employees is generally higher

Consider this example: In the healthcare industry, *cultural competence* as a form of inclusion could potentially have enormous benefit. On a moral level, when cultural considerations are not included in a hospital's overall strategy, it could cost the lives of patients being served. Taking the time to understand how a community's *cultural practices* impact responses to medical treatment may lead to greater effectiveness in how services are offered and accepted.

Based on your organization's unique structure, product or service, core competencies, market positioning and customer cultural make-up, what do you believe would be the most significant advantages that diversity and inclusion would bring to your organization?

Notes on thoughts

Disadvantages

Seldom do leaders discuss the disadvantages of developing a strategy; however, this factor is a critical element to the development of a sound strategy. If you do not discuss the disadvantages and plan for the potential barriers to success, these barriers have the very real potential to derail even the best developed plans and ideas.

There are disadvantages, at least initially, to bringing a diversity and inclusion plan to an organization. Wherever there is a change, productivity could initially drop, revenue may drop, customer satisfaction can initially drop, and teams may find themselves clashing. If you know this could be a potential challenge, you can prepare your organization ahead of the change so they and you are not blindsided. There is wisdom in making every attempt to avert a crash and even then, there is always the danger you may not get to everyone in time to prevent the upset, but you have to try.

Change can always be a challenge in that if not prepared for the downside, when individuals bump up against differences and are not trained how to deal with them, several reactions COULD happen. One, fear takes over and panic sets in. The immediate reaction is to resist and protect what was and keep the familiar the way it is. Some people would rather dance with the devil they know than the devil they don't know because at least they know this devil. Status quo, even if it is horrible, is what is known and human nature being what it is, people will go to amazing lengths to keep what they know in place rather than allow it to be changed.

Another choice people make when they bump up against change is to do nothing. They do not know what to do or how to behave so they do not do anything. They become passive and just let the matter drop. That way they cannot be accused of doing the wrong thing, saying the wrong thing, or behaving in an inappropriate manner. If they do not respond, then they cannot be accused of improper or unacceptable conduct. Finally, a third choice is to do something based on past experience which is often woefully inadequate and erroneous, but it is the best choice the individual can make at that time. Tempers flare, feelings get hurt, and the situation could end up worse had no one tried to do anything.

These are but a sample of the disadvantages of creating a strategy of diversity and inclusion for your organization. You have to have an honest conversation with your leadership team and representative employee groups so that you may flush out the potential advantages AND disadvantages of your diversity and inclusion strategy. You can then be clear on what to expect. Only then can you determine how best to deal with these issues for your organization.

Again, given your in-depth knowledge of your organization's intricate underpinnings and unwritten rules in how the culture functions, ask yourself:

- What are the most significant disadvantages diversity and inclusion may bring to this organization?
- How will you deal with these disadvantages?
- What message(s) does the culture express when visitors view your website?
- What message(s) may be received by visitors to your office when they are in the lobby?
- What might others be seeing when they view your marketing materials?

Notes on thoughts

Internal Factors:

As you begin to think about the internal factors that are pulling your organization, keep in mind change can be emotionally exhausting and what you are asking your organization to do may get harder before it gets easier. So keep this in mind. Be a realist about this strategy. Ask yourself some questions:

- What internal factors are pulling the organization to change?
- What direction are you being pulled into?
- Are you structured to maximize external opportunities?
- Are your corporate policies focused on sustaining long term success? How so?
- Who do your policies (written or unwritten) exclude?
- Do you maintain outdated policies that are no longer meaningful or useful?
- Are your internal organizational behaviors perceived by your members as exclusive to certain groups? How do you know?
- Is your organization growing as you want it to grow to meet growing customer demands?
- Do you have the infrastructure to make this happen? Are you planning to become a global organization?
- Does your organization look like and behave like an inclusive organization? How do you know?
- How will you *pull* your customer demands through your organization as it is now?
- Up until now, what story have you been telling yourselves about yourselves?
- Is this the story that represents your future?
- What do you need to change?

Notes on thoughts

External Forces

The world has changed and organizations have to change their business models to meet customer demands. Customers *push* organizations to change the products they sell, how they sell, and who sells them their products. As you write your strategy for diversity and inclusion, you must be aware of the changing demographics in the markets you are serving and in the marketplace in which you want to compete.

People fear what they don't know and cannot see, which is why it is important to recognize trends and demographic changes that are pushing your organization. Lurking in the corridors of every organization are pockets of resistance that are waiting to link into the network of your organization's structure. If you are not meticulously watching for changes in the marketplace, you could easily be pushed out of the market by the competition because you were not diligent in your observations. Consider these questions:

- Is your organization's ability or inability to change impacting your capacity to compete?
- What external forces are pushing your organization?
- How will you manage these forces?
- What will you do to maintain your competitiveness?
- How do you believe having a diverse and inclusive workplace will help you competitively?
- What are the advantages of the push forces?
- What are the disadvantages of the push forces?

Notes on thoughts

Strategic Success

If you have never designed a diversity and inclusion strategy for your organization, you will need to decide where to begin. The strategy you design should take into consideration where your organization is in its evolution on diversity and inclusion. You may want to start at a basic awareness level and then move on to changing the organization's culture. Whatever you decide, it is critically important that you answer the question, WIIFM (What's in it for me) for everyone in the organization.

Unless employees in the organization believe they have some stake in the outcome or feel some sense of urgency or responsibility in the outcome (ethically or economically), then they have no vested interest in the success of the strategy or the accompanying programs.

- How will you get as many employees as possible vested in the success of this strategy?
- How will you hold leadership accountable and responsible for outcomes?
- How will you hold managers and front line leaders responsible for making this strategy work?
- How will you get employees included and accountable for what they will learn and help make the program a success?
- What will a successfully implemented strategy look like for this organization?

Notes on thoughts

The Time Factor

Let's be clear! Regardless of the size of your team, group, industry, organization or nation, any diversity and inclusion strategy will require **TIME** to be effective. Designing a strategy and expecting the programs to work in three, six, or even 12 months is unrealistic in most instances.

The larger the organization, the longer you should expect it to take for the work of inclusion to move through the organization and for its effect to be seen and felt in the actions, attitudes, and behaviors of its members. Forget the outdated adage that Rome wasn't built in a day and let's talk a bit about growing apples.

According to Waite Maclin of Pastor Chuck's Orchards in Cushing, ME (http://www.pastorchuckorchards.com/index.htm), it can take up to 4-5 years for a new tree to bear fruit, and here is the reason. Today's apple growing strategy is not a simple matter of dropping a seed in the ground and watching a tree grow. In fact, it is quite the opposite of the story you may recall about Johnny Appleseed (John Chapman) traveling across the Midwest planting apple seeds. Growing apple trees is an intentional, calculated process that requires deliberate planning and a good deal of time. Once you have decided the type of apple you want, a cutting of that type of tree is grafted to a rootstock. The rootstock provides the seedling its characteristics such as size, strength, ability to resist disease, and the ability to adapt to the environment. Together, these two pieces, the cutting and the rootstock, create a new seedling, which become the new tree. With nourishment and protection from disease, blight, and insects, it can take up to 5 years for the tree to bear fruit.

So what in the world does growing apples have to do with designing an effective diversity and inclusion strategy? Here's the point! A diversity and inclusion strategy in an organization may be compared to grafting a seedling or growing a new apple tree. Once you decide the type of future you want (seedling) you then graft it to the rootstock (diversity and inclusion strategy). You take care of the seedling and keep it free from disease, blight, and insects (train the organization) so that it is able to grow and bear fruit (inclusion). You get the type of fruit you want and the capacity to grow the organization the way you want based on the conditions set (your original strategy) when the tree is planted in the orchard.

You may have noticed in Figure 1, a conspicuously placed clock representing the element of time. When introducing a strategy into an organization that demands change, in order to be fair in your expectation of success, you must factor time into the strategic equation. Failure to include time as part of your strategic plan may be likened to guaranteeing your plan will not work. As Pastor Chuck says, "Eternal watchfulness is mandatory" and not just in regard to apples. Eternal watchfulness is necessary when implementing diversity and inclusion programs as well.

Notes on thoughts

Putting the Diversity and Inclusion
Strategic Plan Together

You have had the opportunity to incorporate your vision, mission and values into a diversity and inclusion vision and mission statement. You have also considered the advantages, disadvantages of the strategy you are planning for your organization. The factor of time has been included in your plan and now you need to put it all together. The following pages are for you to put your diversity and inclusion strategy together. Follow the instructions on each page being careful to take into consideration how each goal will help you create the type of future you want for your organization.

The Diversity and Inclusion Strategic Plan Worksheet: Putting the Strategy Together

Vision: _____

Mission: _____

Governing Values: _____

List all of your strategic goals keeping in mind your vision, mission, and governing values. Ask:

- What are the best choices we can make that align with the overall vision?
- How do these goals align with the overall mission of the organization?
- How will these D&I goals help the organization create the future we envision?

Goal #1 _____

Goal #2 _____

Goal #3 _____

Goal #4 _____

Goal #1

Diversity and Inclusion Plan by Goal

Description

Objective(s)
- _____
- _____
- _____

Major Activities / Timeline	Q1	Q2	Q3	Q4
• _____				
• _____				
• _____				

Key Performance Indicators (measuring effectiveness)
- _____
- _____
- _____

Organizational Learning: How can we share best practices and successes across the organization, the community, and all stakeholders?

- _____
- _____
- _____

Goal #2

Diversity and Inclusion Plan by Goal

Description _____

Objective(s)
- _____
- _____
- _____

Major Activities / Timeline	Q1	Q2	Q3	Q4
• _____				
• _____				
• _____				

Key Performance Indicators (measuring effectiveness)

- _____
- _____
- _____

Organizational Learning: How can we share best practices and successes across the organization, the community, and all stakeholders?

- _____
- _____
- _____

Goal #3

Diversity and Inclusion Plan by Goal

Description

Objective(s)

- _____
- _____
- _____

Major Activities / Timeline	Q1	Q2	Q3	Q4
• _____ • _____ • _____				

Key Performance Indicators (measuring effectiveness)

- _____
- _____
- _____

Organizational Learning: How can we share best practices and successes across the organization, the community, and all stakeholders?

- _____
- _____
- _____

Goal #4

Diversity and Inclusion Plan by Goal

Description
_____

Objective(s)
- _____
- _____
- _____

Major Activities / Timeline	Q1	Q2	Q3	Q4
• _____ • _____ • _____				

Key Performance Indicators (measuring effectiveness)
- _____
- _____
- _____

Organizational Learning: How can we share best practices and successes across the organization, the community, and all stakeholders?

- _____
- _____
- _____

Phase II: Designing the Strategy Wrap-up

- Why is this strategy the best plan for your organization?

_____

_____

_____

_____

_____

_____

_____

- Does your vision and mission unite your organization around your purpose?

_____

_____

_____

_____

_____

- How will you monitor changing trends that could impact your strategy?

_____

_____

_____

_____

_____

_____

Phase III - Implementing Your Diversity and Inclusion Program

Once the strategy has been designed, it is important to deliver programs that build the skill set organizational members will need to develop in order to deliver on the vision and make the mission a reality. Building the skill set generally requires training, and training involves using the organization's two precious resources, time and money. The programs selected **MUST** be aligned with the strategy and be in sync with the needs of the organization's stated mission. This may be implemented in phases, steps, quarterly, weekly, or monthly. However you decide to deliver these programs, the purpose must be clear and consistently communicated.

The plan for delivery should be clearly laid out after getting as many levels of the organization involved as possible. Representatives from all levels of leadership, management and employees should be involved in the implementation phase. This will keep those impacted in the know, involved, and participating. Keeping as many members involved as possible also lessens the shock to the system as they are able to keep everyone at their level in the know regarding the events about to transpire.

There is clearly a difference between effective and efficient delivery of any program. If you are only concerned with efficient delivery then you will want to do the least possible in order to get something done. There is nothing wrong with this approach when cost is your first concern. Efficiency is about ensuring there is as little waste as possible. This approach makes good business sense; however, this approach should not be the ONLY approach.

An effective training approach should also be considered when implementing a new strategy. Being effective means being able to produce desired results in a way that gives power to the end results. This is the effect you want your diversity and inclusion program to have on your organization. You want your diversity and inclusion program to have the power to create a new way of organizational life that does not now exist. Efficiently and effectively using the power of strategically designed programs that are aligned with overall corporate goals and integrated into every business unit provides the opportunity to create a new *meme* for your leadership, your organization, and your community.

- When considering how you will deal with resistance, who has the most to gain from keeping the status quo?
- How might you make this strategy meaningful for this group of individuals as well?
- How will you get and keep them involved?
- How will you get them focused on their purpose and future possibility?

Notes on thoughts

Communicating the Message

Here is where you will really get to show you mean what you say. As leader, how you deliver your message to your organization is critical. There are many media you may use; however, the first and most important message must come from you. Your message must resonate with your organization. You want it to be *memorable* and *sticky* yet believable and meaningful. Presenting your members with a powerful, moving, logical reason why this strategy makes sense is critical. Most important, your audience must see themselves in the story you are telling about the future of the organization. This is important: Your story cannot be perceived as fake or contrived. The organization's membership must connect with you and what you say.

As you reflect on the many opportunities to understand and respect differences, you will want to carefully evaluate what areas of the organization need specific training and development to address opportunities for growth. Diversity and inclusion training should align with overall corporate strategies and be included within the strategies of every business unit. Suggestions for inclusion training include development training that facilitates learning how to grow the following *fruits of inclusion*™:

- Enter into honest dialogue
- Grow trust-based relationships
- Constructively manage conflict
- Demonstrate real respect for differences
- Create a safe space for saying no to the status quo
- Consistently work toward mutual understanding
- Create a sense of community
- Create win-win approach to problem solving
- Engage in cooperative decision making
- Establish clearly defined ethical boundaries
- Experience equity-based justice for all members
- Engaged commitment from employees who choose to get involved

In general, when these 12 fruits of inclusion are consistently being practiced within any organization, regardless of the industry, you can be assured that inclusion has been born and the fruits of inclusion have become standard practice (meme) within the psychological space of the organization.

Questions you may consider:

- What message do you want to send?
- What media will you use?
- How will you frame your communication program?
- What is the most effective message you can consistently send about second generation diversity and inclusion training?

Notes on thoughts

In-House Trainers and Consultants

Given the plethora of training programs on the market, the prudent and wise consumer will combine the need to be efficient with the need to be effective when searching for the best way to deliver the strategy. Let's be clear… training is going to cost… great training is going to cost more… **poor training costs the MOST**!

When in-house delivery is one of the considerations, consider a *train the trainer* program from a consultant who has a deep level of expertise and could deliver training that is practical, useable, and will be well received. While trainer styles will and should vary, there should be a core curriculum and information that should be consistent. Everyone should get the same message. Keep in mind, both in-house and external consultants can work together for the benefit of the organization. When working together, these individuals are not competitors; but are partners working on behalf of the organization.

If you are thinking of going outside, then you may want to see if there are local consulting organizations that fit the level of expertise you need AND who would be able to manage the amount of training you want to deliver. Generally, local consultants have a vested interest in seeing the community grow and evolve as a diverse and inclusive organization. This is not to suggest national organizations would not do a good job… some would; however, the commitment to the community just might not be as strong. Finding local consultants is not always possible or feasible. The depth of expertise is not always available at the local level.

When it is not in the best interest of the organization to proceed at the local level, it is important to select a consultant or team of consultants who have depth of expertise, a history of successfully delivering the types of programs you need, and provide solid recommendations as to their ability to deliver what they say they can. In making your decision, always keep the best interest of your organization in mind, as well as your stated objectives.

Ask yourself:

- Who will be responsible for managing training?
- What skill-based training do you need that will support your inclusion strategy?
- What does success in skill-based training look like for your organization?
- Who needs to be trained? On what will you base the need to be trained?
- Where are your most pressing training needs in the organization?
- Where do you begin?
- How will you deliver this training? (Webinars, online, classroom, video, self-paced, etc.)
- How will you track who attends training?
- How will you track progress of participants?
- What other factors do you need to consider?

Notes on thoughts

Some obstacles to Effective Diversity and Inclusion Training

Another factor to consider is to know upfront what issues could cause the diversity and inclusion strategy to be less successful than you planned. No one can implement a program successfully without considering the ways things could go wrong or what causes diversity and inclusion programs to fail or not work as well as they could. Consider some of these obstacles (you may also want to consider some of your own distinctive barriers based on your organization's unique issues).

- Failure to get the highest level leader involved in the beginning
- A general lack of accountability
- Failure to incorporate skill-based inclusion training into the strategy
- Failure to deal with the disadvantages of diversity strategies
- Only providing training because a negative event occurred
- Failure to align diversity training to overall corporate learning or strategic goals
- Misunderstanding what diversity and inclusion mean to everyone, not just a select few
- Not addressing negative attitudes or misunderstandings about diversity
- Focusing on shame, guilt, and blame
- Failure to include follow up strategies
- Failure to hold leadership accountable
- Focusing only on the business case for diversity and not the ethical or moral basis for diversity and inclusion
- Failure to acknowledge diversity and inclusion takes time, effort, resources and commitment

- Failure to help employees see themselves in the diversity strategy
- Failure to make it clear why diversity and inclusion strategies are necessary
- Failure to make it safe for honest dialogue or to teach the difference between honest discussions and mean-spirited conversations
- Ignoring the culture – written policies don't run organizations, unwritten rules do
- Failure to embrace the true fruits of inclusion

These are a few of the potential derailing barriers that research has suggested could get in the way of even the best laid plans.

- What are some of the barriers that are unique to your organization?

- How will you address these issues?

- What do you want to avoid happening in this organization?

- What do you want to be sure does happen?

Notes on thoughts

Diversity and Inclusion Training Programs Worksheet

Department / Functional Area: _____

Manager / Inclusion Champion: _____

Needs Analysis: _____ Yes _____ No

Type of Training needed (see samples below):

❏ Communication skills	❏ Team building	❏ Leader development
❏ Conflict management	❏ Diversity awareness	❏ Managing differences
❏ Management skills	❏ Decision-making	❏ Problem-solving
❏ Ethics program	❏ Stress Management	❏ The Art of Storytelling

Other programs:

_____

_____

_____

How will this training align with the diversity and inclusion strategy?

_____

_____

_____

What is the potential impact of NOT training the organization in these skills?

_____

_____

_____

Preferred training media?

❏ Classroom	❏ Online / self-paced	❏ Local university
❏ Webinars	❏ Use Consultants	❏ Coaching

Other considerations:
- Budget
- Time Constraints
- Metrics and evaluations
- Benchmarks
- Impact to the organization
- Sharing of best practices
- Required technology

Phase III: Implementing Your Diversity and Inclusion Program Wrap-up

- What training programs hold the most promise for creating a culture of inclusion?

- How will you continue to hold yourself and others accountable for continuous development of programs that support the strategy?

- As you bring people together in trusting relationships, what challenges might you expect? How will you deal with these challenges?

- Are you encouraging employee involvement and participation in the process?

Phase IV – Accountability, Evaluation, and Sustaining Results

Accountability, evaluation, and sustainability are three factors that must be considered in the final phase of designing a successful strategy.

Accountability

Accountability is being responsible and answerable for outcomes. It is explaining why a strategy did or did not work. Accountability is evaluating and critiquing what went well and what did not go as well as it should have and being able to provide an honest evaluation of how to fix or alter outcomes to move in the desired direction. Accountability means someone is responsible for ensuring that measurements are put in place that clearly demonstrate what is being done to deliver the anticipated results and if not, then explanation should be provided why results are not as expected.

In order to be accountable, there must be clear and specific metrics that will be measured. To be sure you have the best people doing the best they can to implement the best strategy you can possibly develop, measurements must be in place with someone responsible for ensuring the work is being done and is being done according to plan.

Generally, a diversity and inclusion strategy that includes training programs for all functional areas of an organization is evaluated from the bottom up as well as the top down. This means that everyone with a seat gets a say. Most organizations are well-accustomed to top down evaluations, but very seldom are organizations prepared for or accustomed to bottom-up feedback. Imagine if students were able to grade their teachers! What grades do you think most teachers would get? Do you think it would revolutionize how teachers would teach? Of course it would! The teaching profession might lose a lot of teachers, but it could open up a world of possibility that those who genuinely love the profession of teaching would be free to really teach students so that they are able to really learn. Let's apply this analogy to diversity and inclusion.

It can be frightening to open the possibility that disgruntled or unhappy employees will have an opportunity to have a say in their manager's performance review, or that managers may have some impact on their boss's review. However, given the urgency of the state of organizations, don't you think it is about time someone changed how the process is currently being done? Does it take courage to implement a diversity and inclusion strategy that could really work? Does it take real work and considerable thought? Will it take genuine change in how the organization is being operated? The answer to all of these questions is an unequivocal and resounding YES!

Evaluating Progress

Report Card / Progress Report

Remember when you had to take your report card home? When you had great grades, you ran home to show your parents and your grandparents because you wanted everyone to know you worked hard and got good marks. When you did not do so well, you were more hesitant to show off your grades. The same principle applies to your diversity and inclusion progress report card. As an organization, it is important to know where you stand. If you tell the organization where you are in sales revenues or other strategy plans, then the diversity and inclusion plan should be no different.

One of the great things about technology today is that you can create your own progress report card system. You may make it as elaborate or as simple as you would like but it is important for you to have one. There are also commercial grading systems available for you to purchase. The choice is yours. Whatever decision you make on the type of report card you select, you will want to consider whether you make the grading system public or private.

Grading system

You should ALWAYS know where you are going and ALWAYS know where you stand (grade yourself and let others evaluate your successes or failure). When you are serious about what you are doing, you will show the world your grade. If you get a B then you get a B. If you get an F then you get an F but at least you know where you stand and you can now DO SOMETHING about where you are. Fear only exacerbates what you already know is not working. A system of evaluation is not be meant to punish but to offer opportunities for continued development in growing inclusive cultures.

The example (Figure 2) below is just one way an organization may put together a progress report to evaluate how their strategy is or is not progressing.

Leader:_____ **Business Unit:**_____

Dimension	Comments	Progress (Select one rating for each dimension)		
		☐ Above Average	☐ Average	☐ Below Average
Engages in honest dialogue				
Builds trusting relationships				
Manages conflict well				
Respects differences				
Makes it safe to say no				
Promotes mutual understanding				
Creates a sense of community				
Win/win problem solving				
Cooperative decision making				
Clear ethical boundaries				
Equity-based justice				
Employees are engaged and committed				

Figure 2

Measurements

Generally organizations look at metrics quarterly. Your leadership team should be clear on what will be measured and who will be measuring them. Research suggests that companies with the most success for diversity and inclusion programs regularly report their survey results and progress reports to their employees in a public forum such as their company website along with their diversity vision and mission statement. This clear statement of diversity and inclusion makes a public statement of the organization's seriousness to be inclusive.

- How will you measure your organization's success of your unique diversity and inclusion strategies?
- Will you measure leaders on all of the performance indicators or the top 3 -5 based on your organization's specific objectives?
    - ○ Retention
    - ○ Customer Satisfaction ratings
    - ○ Productivity and quality performance ratings
    - ○ Employee satisfaction surveys
    - ○ Leadership satisfaction surveys
    - ○ Decrease in employee complaints and harassment suits or legal actions
- What are the key performance metrics you will be using?
- How often will your leaders be measured?
- Who will measure how well your leaders / managers are doing (bottom up and top down?)
- How will you measure for the organization's progress?
- Will community partners have a say in how well they believe your organization is doing in accomplishing the strategy? If so, when?
- Will you measure skill development?
- At the macro level how will you attach goals to organizational performance objectives?
- At the micro level how will you establish team goals and individual performance?

Notes on thoughts

Sustainability

If you do not want to lose your resources and all of your efforts in the abyss of nothingness, you need to incorporate the factor of sustainability into your strategic design and into the development of your training programs that will support the strategy. Sustainability is about maintaining, supporting, *and nourishing* the strategy and the programs produced by the strategy to keep it alive. As previously discussed, making inclusion

sustainable requires making a major shift in attitudes, attention, and focus in how diversity and inclusion are managed and by whom. Inclusion must be distinguished from diversity and a climate of trust encouraged at every level within the organization in order to thrive.

Milestones are an important part of making any strategy work. Milestones are markers or posts along the road that tell you where you are in the journey. These milestones may serve as indicators of good or not so good things going on. Keep in mind that because there are some disadvantages to diversity and inclusion, you need to know what they are so that when you see them, you don't become derailed. With training comes awareness and with awareness comes power to deal with the known. What you know and understand and have been trained to deal with you can most likely handle. Likewise, when you see the positive milestones, celebrate even the smallest victory because they are signs of greater good to come. Milestones, both positive and negative, can be important when you know what they mean and how to deal with them.

Diversity and inclusion must become a part of the culture and be included in everyday conversation as part of the sustainability effort. Keep in mind, diversity is the seed, inclusion is the fruit and it may take a while to grow the seedling into a tree that will bear the fruit you want. This requires staying power. In the meantime, you must monitor the results of the efforts of leadership, middle managers, front line supervision, employees and every stakeholder.

Ask yourself:

- How will you secure participation in the process of inclusiveness?
- How will you recognize improvements in organizational performance?
- What will a change in attitude toward respecting differences look like?
- What will a change toward an organizational climate of inclusion feel like?
- Since retention is important, why are employees leaving and what can or should be done about it?
- Is creative problem solving occurring and ideas being submitted or are they being ignored?
- Are issues in teams being worked out on their own or is intervention necessary and is it helpful?
- Are quality of work standards improving?
- Are team members demanding higher standards of each other?
- Are there team goals that facilitate cooperation and a healthy competitive spirit or is antagonism and back stabbing encouraged?
- Are leaders at every level encouraging structured deviance as a way of encouraging inclusion and generating new ideas?
- Are open and honest discussions used as a way of leading change and growing strategies that develop fresh approaches to old problems?
- Are all stakeholders encouraged by the sense of community that comes with inclusiveness in a climate of trust?
- How will you continue to monitor changing demographics and trends that could impact how your strategy may be adjusted as necessary?
- How will you adjust what is not working, continue what is, and how often will you need to evaluate and readjust?
- How should you reward the behavior you want to continue?
- How will you sanction the behavior you don't want to spread?

Notes on thoughts

Another way to sustain a strategy and the programs tied to it is to create visible partnerships within the organization where individuals at every level within the organization (and partners that are outside but have a vested interest in the organization's success) have some authority and support from leadership such as:

- Employee councils
- Affinity groups
- Diversity and inclusion policy makers
- Diversity and inclusion resource center with reading material, DVDs, access to information to learn about other cultures
- Formal mentoring programs including reverse mentoring programs
- Monthly / quarterly programs that help the organization discover and understand other cultures and how little is known about each other
- Succession plans that fill the pipelines with diverse candidates from varying cultures with varying backgrounds and differences
- Internship programs, summer programs, cooperative programs in partnerships with local high schools, vocational schools, community colleges
- Incentive programs that recognize and reward behaviors you want replicated
- Specially trained Inclusion Program Managers (that are trained to watch trends, best practices, develop new and exciting programs, etc.)
- Inclusion Coaches
- Supplier diversity goals that are real and meaningful

These are but a few suggestions for organizations to use. There are many ways, both large and small businesses may get people inspired to work together creating the future they want to be a part of. The leader's role is to create the type of culture where this kind of motivational energy and commitment to the greater good, while bringing economic security for all, may be realized. This is one way you know diversity and inclusion is working!

Notes on thoughts

Dealing with Change

Where you sit very often determines what you see. For many, dealing with the issues of diversity and inclusion is about dealing with personal issues of deeply held beliefs, values, and assumptions that have long been left unchallenged and unchanged, leaving many not seeing the need to do anything different. Changing others is an illusion. In reality, we can only change ourselves. We may choose to behave as others expect or we may choose to empower ourselves. We know we get what we focus on and we can only fix what we can acknowledge.

Changing behavior is easier when you understand where a behavior originated and what purpose it served. It can then be replaced. This usually means we have to replant, reseed or weed out unnecessary, outdated, and unhelpful attitudes, behaviors, beliefs, and values, and then *loosely* repot our psychological containers in order to create cultures of inclusion… not just for someone else, but mostly for ourselves. Too many of us find this uncomfortable and worse yet, don't think we even need to go through the exercise. Even more of us think that because we are not mean to other people, we don't have a problem with differences. Diversity and inclusion are about a deep change in attitudes that drive behaviors. If you are struggling with the concepts of diversity and inclusion but are serious about aerating the *soil of assumptions* and changing how you view diversity and inclusion, respond to these questions:

- Is fear the motivation behind my behaviors and beliefs?
- Am I so driven by past experiences I cannot see truth beyond my own normal conditioning?
- Have I allowed other influences to impact my perspectives of what inclusion could offer?
- Am I disowning the issues around diversity and inclusion?
- What can I do to overcome my uncomfortableness with diversity and inclusion?
- Do I feel safe in asking for help in exploring my perceptions and values about this subject?
- Can I change my conversation on this subject to one that is more helpful and anticipatory of good results?

Sometimes the cold hard truth is I need to change. So why don't I? Here's why (you will have to come up with your own):

Why I don't change:

- I am more attracted to another value
- I am too focused on the past
- I cannot see beyond the present and I get fearful about tomorrow
- I don't want to go "out of bounds" – (Reality is widely accepted and I don't want to go out bounds)
- Don't want to deal with the real issue
- Don't see WIIFM (what's in it for me)
- Lack understanding of the real issue
- Fearful of being inadequate
- In bondage to the present behavior

Now it is your turn:
Why you are resistant to change:

_____

_____

_____

_____

_____

_____

_____

_____

_____

_____

_____

_____

_____

_____

_____

_____

_____

_____

_____

_____

_____

_____

_____

_____

Here is why I believe my organization is resistant to change:

_____

_____

_____

_____

_____

_____

_____

_____

_____

_____

_____

_____

_____

_____

_____

_____

_____

_____

_____

_____

_____

_____

_____

_____

_____

_____

_____

Here are some personal suggestions for overcoming some of that resistance:

Notes on thoughts

Phase IV: Accountability, Evaluation, and Sustaining Results Wrap-up

- How will you continue to hold yourself and others accountable for continuous development of programs that support the strategy?

_____

_____

_____

_____

_____

_____

_____

_____

- As you consider the metrics by which you will be evaluated, what fears will you have to face?

_____

_____

_____

_____

_____

_____

_____

_____

_____

_____

_____

_____

- Will you be able to expect the best from others? Why or why not?

_____

_____

_____

_____

_____

_____

_____

_____

_____

_____

- As you evaluate your progress, how will you collaborate on best practices?

_____

_____

_____

_____

_____

_____

_____

_____

_____

_____

_____

_____

Conclusion

Given the multicultural society we find ourselves a part of, it has become the responsibility of each of us to make inclusion and diversity work. We have to acknowledge our fears and ignorance and break the bonds that are holding our perceptions prisoner to outdated values and beliefs. If we hold on to our fears, our shame, our inability to look forward, we are in essence condemning ourselves to stagnation, entropy, and ultimately the death of creativity, innovation, and acceptance not only for others but for ourselves as well.

Take the time to look through your psychological container and challenge yourself to be honest, candid and open about what you see there. Ask yourself if your beliefs are still relevant in today's society, if there could be other explanations, and how you came to believe what you believe about others. When it comes to making diversity and inclusion work, we have to be unreasonable (go beyond our normal limits). Reason says we follow standards, traditions, and what is known. If I want to be respected for who I am then I must respect others as well. Diversity and inclusion run both ways and not in a single direction. Ask yourself, how can I easily make diversity and inclusion work for all of us? When you ask these types of questions you direct your focus on your future state and where you want to be; not where you were.

When attempting to understand how inclusion helps all of us it is important to remember, not only do we live up to people's expectations... we live down to them too. If we do not expect much of others, we won't get much from them. It matters less what the message is I think I send. What matters most is the message received. So whether we believe we can or cannot build an organization of inclusiveness, commitment, and engaging diversity... either way we are correct. The messages we send are most often grounded in our personal belief and value systems.

We are not all weak in the same places; nor are we all strong in the same ways. It is because of our differences that we need each other. None of us are as strong as all of us. Together we build a foundation of support that makes our differences our strengths.

One may never know the extent of the power found in reframing beliefs about *self* or *others,* but it is clear that if one takes the time to examine closely guarded and long held values, assumptions, and beliefs about one's self and others, new truths are likely to emerge.

We are all diverse and we all want to be included! So now, how do we get to the next level? We take ourselves there. Whenever we change something or do something new, we create neural pathways which make it easier the next time we do that activity. We have to mentally create neural pathways for inclusion to succeed. We have to see ourselves being inclusive and accept our own diversity and the diversity of others. This in turn will build stronger neural pathways, stronger resolutions to be our best and we will be building stronger organizations.

Our beliefs tend to control just about everything about our behaviors. Sometimes we are blinded by our own beliefs and values to the exclusion of seeing new paths that would light our way. There is a story told (author unknown) of a man who was looking for his keys. He was looking for them under the bright street light. His neighbors saw him and came out to help him find his keys. Finally one neighbor asked him where he lost his keys. The man said, "Inside my house." Stunned, the neighbor then asked, "Then why are you looking for them out here?" The man said, "Because there is more light out here."

Now we may laugh at this silly man who was blinded by his beliefs, but how many of us are equally blinded by beliefs about others that are just as silly... just as negative... and just as useless? If we are not being a part of the solution, we are part of the problem. Are you part of your organization's problems?

We don't have to be blind to differences, nor should we be, because we are not all the same. It is the recognition of each other's differences that makes us strong. We have to see what makes us different in order to acknowledge, accept, and ultimately understand each other.

Diversity and inclusion are not for the faint of heart. It takes courage to stand up and be counted for truly valuing differences; not just giving lip service. We have to make conscious choices every day to choose inclusion rather than the status quo or compliance and not let the element of time deter you.

Remember… diversity and inclusion strategies and programs are not quick fixes. Time is a key factor that must be kept in mind. You are growing organizations much like apple orchards and this kind of growth takes time, but the payoff is almost always delicious!

Notes on thoughts

FRUITS OF INCLUSION

TM 2007

Sidebar: The Concept of the Fruits of Inclusion

The concept of the fruits of inclusion has been repeated throughout this workbook. This deserves some additional attention as it is the essential factor to effectively making diversity work for everyone. *We are all already diverse.* What we don't need is more diversity... what we need is to learn how to make our diversity succeed together and that comes through the work of inclusion. In order for inclusion to be able to work, it has to have an opportunity to grow and in order to grow, it has to have a chance for the seed to be planted and its germination to take place. Then the plant of inclusion must be nurtured, fed, and cared for so it does not die. From the *birth of inclusion*™ come the fruits of inclusion™ which are:

- Honest dialogue
- Trust based relationships
- Constructively managed conflict
- Real respect for differences
- Safe spaces for saying no
- Mutual understanding
- Sense of community
- Win-win approaches to problem solving
- Cooperative decision making
- Clearly defined ethical boundaries
- Equity based justice
- Engage and secure commitment

When these twelve factors, which are not exclusive unto themselves, are present in any team, group, or organization, you will find inclusion has been born and is thriving and well.

Here is what happens in many organizations that explains why inclusion efforts often fail. When we do not know how to deal with differences, conflicts occur, as they do in everyday encounters, some type of reaction immediately takes place. Many times people do not know how to respond to the difference they encounter so they react negatively without even knowing it. Other times, the reaction is to do nothing out of fear of responding inappropriately. Yet another way of responding is through a knee-jerk response based on past experiences without enough information which leads to negative responses, depending on the other person or the situation. Finally, a person who has been skill-based trained to recognize and understand how to respond to differences and reacts appropriately is more likely to have a more positive and rewarding experience when dealing with differences. It is when we bump up against differences and do not know what to do that we get in trouble. Giving birth to inclusion is a way to help move beyond one's fear of differences and the illogical resistance to the fear of being changed by others' definition of diversity.

Political correctness is the antithesis of honest dialogue in that it encourages dishonest, impolite, and often disingenuous conversations and behavior. The term *political correctness* appears to have as much baggage around it as the word diversity. The term now seems to be used by some as an excuse to be rude and hateful and when used in this context, gets in the way of genuine and honest dialogue. How words are used and in what context they are used should be understood and clearly defined.

Giving birth to inclusion negates the need for political correctness in that it overrides irrational fears that no one is safe with each other's differences. Inclusion helps us finally get the courage to open the luggage that has been carried around in what we do when no one sees and what is said when no one hears and how one behaves when they believe they are safe. Birthing and growing inclusion brings people together in ways no other concept can.

When you give yourself permission to get involved and cooperate in practicing the 12 fruits of inclusion, the results of your efforts will make organizations, communities, society, and the nation a place where differences are respected and where we will find ways to effectively and constructively deal with conflict. Focusing on inclusion will naturally make the acceptance of all our diversity an accepted practice.

Practicing inclusion does not mean harm may never come to another. Inclusion makes it possible to learn from our mistakes. Inclusion means not giving in to fear first. As a concept, inclusion may not be accepted by everyone; however, it is this author's belief that the fruits of inclusion offer unlimited possibilities for the masses. When taught in tandem with *Second Generation Diversity and Inclusion* principles, there are real opportunities for change in organizations of every size and in every industry. Join the *transformers* of organizational learning and begin teaching and practicing the values born in the *fruits of inclusion* and see how your organization may transform!

Personal Action Plan:

What personal commitment are you willing to make to begin practicing the fruits of inclusion?

_____

_____

_____

_____

_____

_____

_____

_____

_____

_____

_____

_____

_____

_____

_____

_____

_____

_____

_____

_____

_____

_____

References

Carroll, L. (1973). *Alice in wonderland* (1st ed.).
New York: Clarkson N. Potter, Inc.

Dawkins, R. (1976). The selfish gene.
USA: Oxford University Press.

Horowitz, F.D. and O'Brien, M. (1989). In the interest of the
nation: A reflective essay on the state of our knowledge
and the challenges before us. *American Psychologist*.
44 (2), 441-445. Retrieved April 2007 from EBSCOHost database.

Maclin, C. W. (2007). *www.pastorchuckorchards.com*

Williams, T. T. (2002). *Red: Passion and patience in the desert.*
Northbrook: Vintage Publishing

Epilogue

Now what? You have been provided a process to develop a concrete diversity and inclusion strategy or ideas to enhance your current programs. What you now do with the information is up to you. As you consider all of your options, please take some time and consider the future of our children living in a diverse and multi-cultural world. Horowitz and O'Brien (1989) stated:

> "We are a nation of diversity. Understanding, respecting, and working in constructive ways with individuals from the diverse cultures that define the United States go beyond the notions of poverty, disadvantage, or even tolerance; a real attempt to understand and appreciate diversity must inform the design of research and social policy. Children are ever the future of a society." (p. 445)

Our children deserve to inherit the best possible future we may create for them. By embracing the concepts offered in *The Fruits of Inclusion*™ we attempt to provide a solid foundation upon which we can build an inclusive society.

If you need assistance in developing your inclusion programs, don't hesitate to ask for help. I wish you the best possible success!

Linda

About the Author

Dr. Linda Burrs is the President and Principal Consultant of the *Step Up to Success!* consulting firm that focuses on leadership and organizational strategies for leaders, teams and individuals. For more than 25 years, Dr. Burrs has brought her rich dynamic approach to the corporate and professional training arena. The breadth of her experience crosses all walks of social and organizational life including law firms, technology organizations, educators, business professionals, leadership groups and non-profit groups.

PHOTO BY DAVE COLEMAN

Dr. Burrs serves on the boards of The Dunbar Institute (Dayton, OH) as Diveristy and Inclusion Director of Programs and on the board of The BenMar Group (New York). She is a founding member of DaytonCoaches.com, an executive, business and career coaching group formed to support individuals in the greater Dayton community who are committed to personal, professional, and organizational growth and development.

Linda designs and delivers targeted and successful coaching interventions and programs designed to *measurably improve personal, leadership and organizational performance.* Her experience, enthusiasm, and high energy provide the foundation for your memorable, life-changing, inspirational experience. When you attend a Step Up To Success! program, you walk away with improved communication skills, better self-management skills, enhanced interpersonal skills and a clearer understanding of your individual strengths and how they contribute to your success both organizationally, professionally, and personally.

Areas of expertise include:
- ⊙ Diversity and Inclusion
- ⊙ Conflict and Relationship Management
- ⊙ Building Inclusive Teams
- ⊙ Effective Communications
- ⊙ Leadership that Transforms
- ⊙ Member ICF (International Coach Federation)
- ⊙ Personal Development and Leadership Coaching

Dr. Burrs is the author of:
- ⊙ **The** Fruits of Inclusion™: A Smart Business Guide to Creating Sustainable Diversity and Inclusion Programs©
- ⊙ The Success Series© (for Executive Leadership, Frontline Managers, Teams and Individuals)
- ⊙ Learning to Groove with the Gremlins©
- ⊙ Diversity: More Than a Notion©
- ⊙ Leaders Behaving Badly©

Contact Information: Dr. Linda J. Burrs
DrBurrs@step-up-to-success.org
P.O. Box 733, Miamisburg, OH 45343-0733
Office: 937-866-7511 — Fax: 937-866-7512
www.step-up-to-success.org OR www.DrBurrs.com